HOW
TO BE
HAPPY
THOUGH
MARRIED

MATRIMONIAL STRIFE THROUGH THE AGES

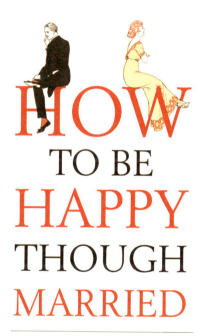

HOW
TO BE
HAPPY
THOUGH
MARRIED

MATRIMONIAL STRIFE THROUGH THE AGES

· OLD HOUSE ·

First published in Great Britain in 2013 by Old House books & maps,
Old House Books, PO Box 883, Oxford OX1 9PL, UK.
PO Box 3985, New York, NY 10185-3985, USA.
Website: www.oldhousebooks.co.uk

A CIP catalogue record for this book is available from the British Library.
ISBN-13: 978 1 90840 258 5

Compiled by Emily Brand.

Images are acknowledged as follows:
The British Library Board, pages 46, 75, 83, 127, 132
The Bridgeman Art Library, page 10
David Cory, pages 16 and 39
Sally Edelstein, pages 79, 94, 111 and 139
Lewis Walpole Library, Yale University, pages 30, 53, 58, 90, 129, 135 and 143.
Mary Evans Picture Library, cover illustration, pages 15, 27, 34, 63, 67, 68, 70, 87, 102, 114, 118, 122

Printed in China through Worldprint Ltd.

13 14 15 16 17   10 9 8 7 6 5 4 3 2 1

To those brave men and women who have ventured, or who intend to venture, into that state which is "a blessing to a few, a curse to many, and a great uncertainty to all", this book is respectfully dedicated in admiration of their courage.

CONTENTS

A NOTE FROM THE EDITOR

"Keep your eyes wide open before marriage,
half shut afterwards."
– *Benjamin Franklin (1706–1790)*

As any brave soul who has ventured into the perilous world of romance will know, true love is a most dangerous beast – and especially so when we attempt to shackle it in the chains of wedlock.

The present volume – being a compendium of matrimonial counsels from the last three thousand years – is intended as a guide and a gift to those who have just entered into married life, and to any whose mind is so favourably inclined towards a particular lover that they will likely do so before long.

To those falling in the latter set, I ask this: upon what fond imaginings do you base the notion that your choice shall be a happy one? Have you any solid reason to suppose that your marriage will not simply be another added to the many wretched – nay, catastrophic! – ones which have already taken place?

If you have hitherto been giddy and thoughtless, let this book encourage you to think more carefully on your future, and prevent you from allying yourself to an ale-soaked husband or a nagging wife.

To readers whose opportunity for escape has passed, this guide shall reveal, if not always how to secure domestic harmony, then how best to gain the upper hand in the battle of the sexes. From Ovid to Einstein, and many obscure marriage manuals in between, the age-old secrets of conjugal bliss are here laid before you, including your duties as a spouse and how to keep your partner a willing resident of the marital bed.

The work being both interesting and instructive, I hope you shall be much gratified by its perusal. After all, what can be more pleasing to contemplate than the happy union of two loving human hearts?

That every honourable success, and every consequent happiness, may be the result of your strenuous efforts, is the sincere wish of,

The Editor

Maria Caua donzella dela Uila de Gui
t altra

I

The Pleasures
of Marriage

'What is better than wisdom?
Woman. And what is better than a
good woman? Nothing.'

- GEOFFREY CHAUCER, *THE CANTERBURY TALES*,
14th CENTURY

'Single women have a dreadful propensity for being poor, which is one very strong argument in favour of matrimony.'

- JANE AUSTEN, 1816

'Against love there is no remedy,
neither a potion, nor powder,
nor song; nothing except kissing,
fondling, and lying together naked
are of assistance.'

- LONGUS OF LESBOS, *DAPHNIS AND CHLOE*,
2nd CENTURY AD

'Romantic love is a species
of drunkenness – even dullards
are aware of this; they are aware
of it when they are not in love,
and either forget it or disregard
it when they are.'

- *THE ART OF MAKING A PERFECT HUSBAND*, 1929

'Five or six years of married life will often reduce a naturally irascible man to so angelic a condition that it would hardly be safe to trust him with a pair of wings.'

- HOW TO BE HAPPY THOUGH MARRIED, 1895

'Some reconciliations are attended with such pleasure, that it is almost worth making a quarrel, on purpose for the sake of the joy of a reconcilement.'

- DICTIONARY OF LOVE, 1777

'There is nothing more admirable than when two people who see eye to eye keep house as man and wife, confounding their enemies and delighting their friends.'

- HOMER, *THE ODYSSEY*, *c.* 8th CENTURY BC

'It is a woman's business to get married as soon as possible and a man's to keep unmarried as long as he can.'

- GEORGE BERNARD SHAW,
MAN AND SUPERMAN, 1903

'What an addition to happiness a good wife makes! Such a one is the best companion in prosperity, and in adversity the surest friend; the greatest assistance in business, the only lawful and comfortable means by which she can have issue, and the great remedy against incontinence.'

- *ARISTOTLE'S MASTERPIECE, c.1684*

'Marriage may often be a stormy lake, but celibacy is almost always a muddy horse-pond.'

- THOMAS LOVE PEACOCK, *MELINCOURT*, 1817

'Marriage resembles a pair of shears, so joined that they can not be separated; often moving in opposite directions, yet always punishing anyone who comes between them.'

- SYDNEY SMITH, ENGLISH CLERGYMAN (1771–1845)

'There is no road to wealth so easy and respectable as that of matrimony.'

- ANTHONY TROLLOPE, *DOCTOR THORNE*, 1858

II

The Pains
of Marriage

'Love, *n.* A temporary insanity curable by marriage.'

- AMBROSE BIERCE, *THE DEVIL'S DICTIONARY*, 1911

'By all means marry; if you get
a good wife, you'll become happy;
if you get a bad one, you'll become
a philosopher.'

- SOCRATES, 4th CENTURY BC

'Marriage is the tomb of love.'

- GIACOMO CASANOVA (1725–98)

'Marriage is the triumph of imagination over intelligence. Second marriage is the triumph of hope over experience.'

- OSCAR WILDE (1854–1900)

'What fearful disorder must prevail in that domestic circle where the presiding influence of woman is not felt, or where it is felt only as an evil genius exerting a fitful and pernicious control.'

- *COUNSELS TO A NEWLY WEDDED PAIR*, 1836

'It destroys one's nerves to be amiable every day to the same human being.'

- BENJAMIN DISRAELI (1804–81)

'My wife's gone to the country
Hooray! Hooray!
She thought it best, I need a rest,
That's why she's gone away.'

- IRVING BERLIN/GEORGE WHITING,
MY WIFE'S GONE TO THE COUNTRY, 1910

'In old age, marriage is not to be recommended. Two decaying bodies in one bed can never be endured.'

- PHILIP OF NOVARA, *OF THE FOUR AGES OF MAN'S LIFE*, *c.*1265

Coment bel acueil humblement

'Of all the actions of a man's life his marriage doth least concern other people; yet of all actions of our life it is most meddled with by other people.'

- JOHN SELDEN, ENGLISH SCHOLAR (1584–1654)

'Fools are as like husbands
as pilchards are to herrings;
the husband's the bigger.'

- WILLIAM SHAKESPEARE, *TWELFTH NIGHT*

'My wife and I tried to breakfast together, but we had to stop or our marriage would have been wrecked.'

- WINSTON CHURCHILL (1874–1965)

'Advice to persons about to marry.
– "Don't".'

- *PUNCH*, 1845

'There are only two days on which a woman can refresh thee, on the day of marriage and when she is buried.'

- HIPPONAX OF EPHESUS, *c.*540 BC

'Though women are angels,
yet wedlock's the devil.'

- LORD BYRON, *TO ELIZA*

THE SWEET DELIGHTS OF LOVE.

A Smoaky House _ a Failing Trade _ a Squalling Brat _ and a Scolding Jade.

'Bigamy is having one wife too many. Monogamy is the same.'

- OSCAR WILDE (1854–1900)

'Marriage is a lottery, nay the greatest hazard imaginable; an East-India voyage is not half so perilous; thou art made or marred as it proves.'

- *CONJUGIUM CONJURGIUM*, 1673

The Pains of Marriage

'The most happy marriage
I can imagine or picture to
myself would be the union of
a deaf man to a blind woman.'

- SAMUEL TAYLOR COLERIDGE (1772–1834)

'The comfortable estate of widowhood is the only hope that keeps up a wife's spirits.'

- JOHN GAY, *THE BEGGAR'S OPERA*, 1728

'Marriage is a feast where the grace
is sometimes better than the dinner.'

- CHARLES CALEB COLTON,
ENGLISH CLERIC (1780–1832)

'I married beneath me.
All women do.'

- NANCY ASTOR (1879–1964)

'HUSBAND. –
A snarling, crusty, sullen, testy,
forward, cross, gruff, moody,
crabbed, tart, splenetic, surly,
ill-natured, rusty, churlish, growling,
maundering dog in a manger,
who neither eats himself,
nor lets others eat.'

- *DICTIONARY OF LOVE*, 1777

'The "last word" is the most dangerous of infernal machines. Husband and wife should no more fight to get it than they would struggle for the possession of a lighted bomb-shell.'

- *HOW TO BE HAPPY THOUGH MARRIED*, 1895

THE QUARREL.—"If you are not quiet, I will throw this bottle at your head."

'I believe marriages would in general be as happy, and often more so, if they were all made by the Lord Chancellor, upon a due consideration of the characters and circumstances, without the parties having any choice in the matter.'

- SAMUEL JOHNSON (1709–84)

'Marriage is one long conversation,
chequered by disputes.'

- ROBERT LOUIS STEVENSON (1850–94)

'Men marry women with the hope they will never change. Women marry men with the hope they will change. Invariably they are both disappointed.'

- ALBERT EINSTEIN (1879–1955)

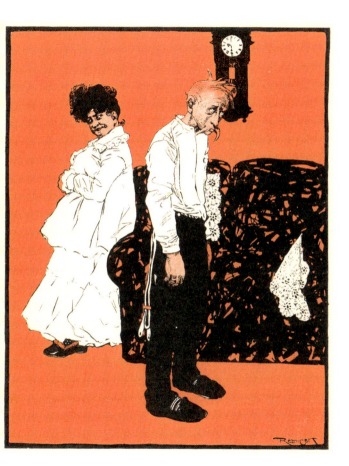

'There are three things that drive a good man from home: a roofless house, a smoky chimney, and a quarrelsome woman.'

- *LE MÉNAGIER DE PARIS*, 1393

III

Hints for Husbands

'According to the old custom, Egyptian women did not wear shoes; this was so that they should spend all day at home. With most women, if you take away their gilded shoes and bracelets and anklets, their purple dresses and their pearls, they too will stay at home.'

- PLUTARCH, *ADVICE TO THE BRIDE AND GROOM,* 1st CENTURY AD

'Don't throw cigar-ends into
the bowl of water your wife keeps
in front of the gas-fire. They are
not ornamental, and she will not
be pleased.'

- DON'TS FOR HUSBANDS AND WIVES, 1913

'One shouldn't be too
inquisitive in life

Either about God's secrets
or one's wife.'

- GEOFFREY CHAUCER, *THE CANTERBURY TALES*,
14th CENTURY

Comment le Jaloux si revient

'He that doth get a wench with child and marries her afterwards it is as if a man should shit in his hat and then clap it on his head.'

- SAMUEL PEPYS, *DIARY*, 1660

'Do not expect her to smile in unmoved serenity when children are ungovernable, servants are in high rebellion, and husband comes home cross and hungry.'

- WEDLOCK, OR THE RIGHT RELATION OF THE SEXES, 1874

'Compliment her new dress,
'hair-do', cooking, etc.'

- SEX TODAY IN WEDDED LIFE, 1947

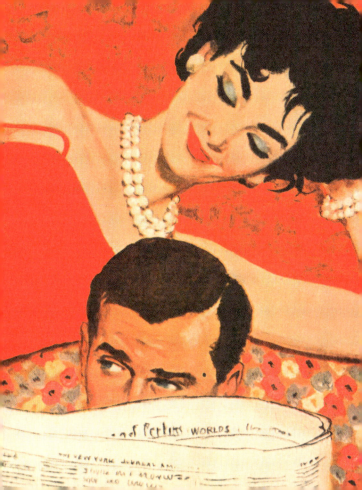

'If you hear her often grunt and groan, mumble and chide, either with the men or maid-servants; nay, you must pass it by, not concerning your self at it.'

- *THE TEN PLEASURES OF MARRIAGE*, 1682

'Cure your unsav'ry breath, gargle your throat; And free your armpits from the ram and goat.'

- OVID, *THE ART OF LOVE*, 1st CENTURY AD

'Remember, if thou marry for beauty, thou bindest thyself all thy life for that which perchance will neither last nor please thee one year; and when thou hast it, it will be to thee of no price at all.'

- SIR WALTER RALEIGH (1552–1618)

'Marrying a stupid woman will prevent you from looking stupid.'

- MOLIÈRE, *L'ÉCOLE DES FEMMES*, *c.* 1662

'I have learned that only two things are necessary to keep one's wife happy. First, let her think she's having her own way. And second, let her have it.'

- LYNDON B. JOHNSON (1908–73)

Hints for Husbands

'When our Mistriss commands us to do anything, nothing should hinder us from giving a blinde obedience.'

- *THE ART OF MAKING LOVE*, 1676

'Should you chance, after dinner, to be affected by a slight drowsiness, never resist it because your wife wishes to chat with you; do not mind her, but go quietly to sleep.'

- 'TO HUSBANDS', *PUNCH*, 1844

'It is not fit that you should already begin to grumble and talk how needfull it is to be sparing and thrifty; that Merchandising and trading is mighty dead; that monies is not to be got in; and that here and there reckonings and bills must be paid: O no! you must be silent, tho' you should burst with discontent.'

- *THE TEN PLEASURES OF MARRIAGE*, 1682

Hints for Husbands

'A BAD HUSBAND -

- Compares wife unfavourably with mother or other wives.

- Publicly praises bachelor days and regrets having married.

- Belches without apology or blows nose at table.

- Teases wife re: fatness, slowness, etc.'

- DR CRANE'S *MARiTAL RATING SCALE*, c.1939

Hints for Husbands

'Never play pranks with your wife,
your horse, or your razor.'

- HINTS FOR LOVERS, 1909

'Do you show your devotion to
a woman by holding her hand or
putting your arm around her when
her friends are present? Please don't.
Even a girl who is affectionate in
private dislikes public mauling.'

- *ESQUIRE'S HANDBOOK FOR HOSTS*, 1954

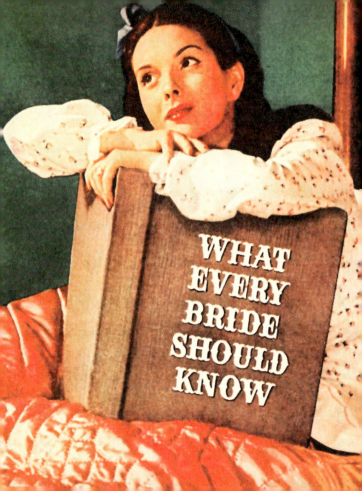

WHAT
EVERY
BRIDE
SHOULD
KNOW

IV

Hints for Wives

'Her hand seeketh employment;
her foot delighteth not in
gadding abroad.'

- THE ECONOMY OF HUMAN LIFE, 1750

'A BAD WIFE -

- Eats onions, radishes or garlic before a date or going to bed.

- Wears pajamas while cooking.

- Fails to wash top of milk bottle before opening it.

- Puts her cold feet on husband at night to warm them.'

- DR CRANE'S *MARITAL RATING SCALE*, *c.*1939

'I consider it every girl's duty to marry £80,000 a year.'

- ALICE CATHERINE MILES, DEBUTANTE, *c.*1868

'The Honeymoon is over;
the die is cast. You and you only
stand between your husband's
and your starvation… Feeding
a husband successfully starts with
feeding him the things he likes
to eat, for a clever bride cooks
to please her man.'

- HAPPY LIVING! A GUIDEBOOK FOR BRIDES, 1965

'Don't sit up till he comes home from the club; better be in bed and pretend to be asleep. If you must be awake, seem to be glad he came home early. He will probably think you an idiot; but that's inevitable anyway.'

- ADVICE IN THE *ISLE OF MAN TIMES*, 1895

'If our husbands are not what we wish – and very few are in every respect – we should try to help them to become so... We are apt to expect too much of manhood even, and hence, instead of a pleasant surprise, experience a sad disappointment.'

- WEDLOCK, 1874

'Don't expect life to be all sunshine.
Besides, if there are no clouds,
you will lose the opportunity
of showing your husband what
a good chum you can be.'

- *DON'TS FOR HUSBANDS AND WIVES*, 1913

'A buxom lass in overalls, with a mannish haircut, rolling a cigarette and handling sacks of fertilizer may be scrupulously scrubbed as clean as a freshly bathed infant. But is she dainty? Definitely not.'

- *LADY, BE LOVED!*, 1953

––◄►◄►––

Hints for Wives

'A true wife should be like a Tortoyse under her shell, ever bearing her house upon her backe.'

- A DISCOURSE OF MARRIAGE AND WIVING, 1615

How to be Happy Though Married

'Be not arrogant and answer not back your husband that shall be, nor his words, nor contradict what he saith, above all before other people.'

- LE MÉNAGIER DE PARIS, 1393

'Instead of running, night after night, to the haunts of fashionable folly, and thus laying the foundation for consumption and a host of fatal diseases, she will retire early, rise with the lark, and find her pleasures in the face of day.'

- A DISCOURSE OF MARRIAGE AND WIVING, 1615

'We remember hearing a husband say that he could always gauge the temper of his wife by the quality of her cooking: good temper even influenced the seasoning of her soups, and the lightness and delicacy of her pastry.'

- *ENQUIRE WITHIN UPON EVERYTHING*, 1856

'I need not warn of too powerful smells,
Which sometimes health or kindly heat expels.
Nor from your tender legs to pluck with care,
The casual growth of all unseemly hair.'

- OVID, *THE ART OF LOVE*, 1st CENTURY AD

'Don't let your husband wear a violet tie with grass-green socks. If he is unhappily devoid of the colour sense, he must be forcibly restrained.'

- DON'TS FOR HUSBANDS AND WIVES, 1913

'Don't grouch before breakfast
– or after it.'

- *THE POPULARITY BOOK*, 1940

'It is doubtful if there is anything more destructive to romance than soiled underwear or body odor.'

- SUCCESSFUL MARRIAGE, 1947

'Before leaving your chamber
or home, be mindful that the collar
of your shift or of your robe does
not slip out one over the other,
as happens with drunken, foolish
or ignorant women who do not care
about their own honour or the
good repute of their estate or
of their husband.'

- LE MÉNAGIER DE PARIS, 1393

Hints for Wives

'Never let your husband have cause to complain that you are more agreeable abroad than at home; nor permit him to see you an object of admiration as respects your dress and manners, when in company, while you are negligent of both in the domestic circle.'

- *MANNERS, CULTURE AND DRESS OF THE BEST AMERICAN SOCIETY*, 1891

'Your first consideration before marriage was, how to please your lover. Consider any such endeavour, after marriage, to be unnecessary and ridiculous; and, by way of amends for your former labour, let your sole object be, to please yourself.'

- 'TO WIVES', IN *PUNCH*, 1844

'Don't imagine that the perfect lover, whether male or female, will come along ready made. If they do, mistrust them, since this shows a certain amount of previous experience.'

- HOW TO BE A GOOD LOVER, 1936

V

The
Marital Bed

'The fate of a marriage depends upon the first night.'

- HONORÉ DE BALZAC (1799–1850)

'I am happy now that Charles calls on my bedchamber less frequently than of old. As it is, I now endure but two calls a week and when I hear his steps outside my door I lie down on my bed, close my eyes, open my legs and think of England.'

- LADY ALICE HILLINGDON, *JOURNAL*, 1912

The Marital Bed

'And she who gluts more than her fill
Of food and wine, soon finds a taste
For bold excess below the waist!
No worthy man will pay his court
To lady of such lowly sort.'

- ROBERT DE BOIS,
ADVICE TO LADIES, 13th CENTURY

'It may not be amiss to remind the bridegroom that the fair lasts all the year, and that he should be careful not to spend his stock lavishly, as women in general are better pleased in having a thing once well done than often ill done.'

- ARISTOTLE'S MASTERPIECE, c. 1684

'When the husband cometh
into his wife's chamber, he must
entertain her with all kinds
of dalliance, wanton behaviour,
and allurements to venery. But if
he perceive her to be slow, and
more cold, he must cherish,
embrace and tickle her.'

*- THE ART OF BEGETTING
HANDSOME CHILDREN, 1860*

How to be Happy Though Married

'A man must hug, and dandle, and kittle, and play a hundred little tricks with his bed-fellow when he is disposed to make that use of her that nature designed her for.'

- THE PRAISE OF FOLLY, 1509

The Marital Bed

'Make good use of your time, and take the full scope of your desires, in the pleasant clasping and caressing of those tender limbs; for after some few daies, hungry care will come and open the Curtains of your bed; and shew you what reckonings you are to expect from the Jeweller, Gold-smith, Silk-man, Linnen-Draper, Vinter, Cook and others.'

- *THE TEN PLEASURES OF MARRIAGE, 1682*

The Marital Bed

'If in the act of copulation, the woman earnestly looks on the man, and fixes her mind on him, the child will resemble the father. Nay, if the woman, even in unlawful copulation, fix her mind upon her husband, the child will resemble him though he did not beget it.'

- ARISTOTLE, *THE NICOMACHEAN ETHICS*, 4th CENTURY BC

'I see silk clothes, if these qualify as clothes, which do nothing to hide the body... Our women have nothing left to show their lovers in the bedroom that they haven't already revealed on the street.'

- SENECA, *DE BENFICIIS*, 1st CENTURY A.D.

'Among the Swahili it is the rule that marriage must not be completely consummated on the wedding night; the bridegroom has only partial connection with his wife, and completes the act with a girl who is at hand for the purpose.'

- *THE MOTHERS*, 1927

⊶•◇•⊷

The Marital Bed

'Legend speaks of the face
that launched a thousand ships;
maybe the one you select
wouldn't even launch a canoe,
but don't let that bother you.'

- *LOOKING TOWARD MARRIAGE*, 1944

'Since the utmost intention
of desire is required in this act,
it may not be amiss for the
bridegroom, for the more eager
heightening of his joy, to delineate
the scene of their approaching
happiness to his fair languishing
bride, in some such amorous
rapture.'

- ARISTOTLE'S MASTERPIECE, c.1684

'In summer take heed that there be no fleas in your chamber, nor in your bed.'

- *LE MÉNAGIER DE PARIS*, 1393

———◦<>◦———

The Marital Bed

'The majority of women (happily for them) are not very much troubled with sexual feeling of any kind.'

- *WILLIAM ACTON*, BRITISH DOCTOR, 1857